HORSES SET II

HIGHLAND PONIES

Kristin Van Cleaf
ABDO Publishing Company

visit us at
www.abdopub.com

Published by ABDO Publishing Company, 4940 Viking Drive, Edina, Minnesota 55435.
Copyright © 2006 by Abdo Consulting Group, Inc. International copyrights reserved in all
countries. No part of this book may be reproduced in any form without written permission from
the publisher. The Checkerboard Library™ is a trademark and logo of ABDO Publishing
Company.

Printed in the United States.

Cover Photo: Corbis
Interior Photos: Animals Animals pp. 5, 11, 13, 23; Corbis pp. 9, 15, 16, 17, 19, 20, 21;
    Peter Arnold pp. 6, 7

Series Coordinator: Heidi M. Dahmes
Editors: Heidi M. Dahmes, Stephanie Hedlund
Art Direction: Neil Klinepier

Library of Congress Cataloging-in-Publication Data

Van Cleaf, Kristin, 1976-
    Highland ponies / Kristin Van Cleaf.
        p. cm. -- (Horses. Set II)
    Includes bibliographical references and index.
    ISBN 1-59679-314-7
    1. Highland pony--Juvenile literature. I. Title.

SF315.2.H5V36 2006
636.1`6--dc22
                                                                2005045737

CONTENTS

WHERE HIGHLAND PONIES CAME FROM

The horse is an old **breed** of animal. In fact, it descends from a small animal called eohippus. This animal lived more than 55 million years ago. But, the horse has grown and changed in many ways since that animal.

Ponies also descend from eohippus. Ponies and horses have similar features and can do many similar things. But, there are a few differences.

The main differences between horses and ponies are size and character. A pony's legs are short compared to its body. A pony is 14.2 hands or under.

One of the best-known ponies is the Highland pony. It is appreciated for its sturdiness, especially in Great Britain. Highland pony bloodlines can be traced to the 1830s. These animals are still popular today.

Highland ponies are popular with pony lovers all around Scotland, England, and other parts of the British Isles.

WHAT HIGHLAND PONIES LOOK LIKE

Highland ponies are the largest of Britain's native pony breeds.

Experts recognize a Highland pony by its distinct features. For example, this pony has a wide forehead. The distance between the eyes and **muzzle** is short. The nostrils are wide. And, the pony has a strong neck.

Ponies are measured in four-inch (10-cm) units called hands. A Highland pony is about 13 to 14.2 hands high. This pony's body is compact. Its hindquarters are very strong. It also has sturdy feet. So, it can travel easily over rough or marshy ground.

This **breed** has short legs with wide knees. The feathery hair on the back of the legs is soft and silky. The tail and mane are flowing and are often left untrimmed.

7

What Makes Highland Ponies Special

The Highland pony is native to the mountains of Scotland. It is able to do many different jobs. Crofters, or small farmers, originally used it to pull carts. Often, Highland ponies were used as pack animals before roads were built.

Highland ponies have also done important work in Scotland. In 1955, they began pony trekking. Their quiet nature and ability to carry a lot of heavy items made them perfect for the job.

Today, Highland ponies still work in the hills of Scotland. They are used for riding and driving. And, they are good family ponies. Highlands are a favorite of people in many parts of the world.

Highland ponies are used to transport logs and carry deer carcasses. Wearing a special packsaddle, the ponies can transport a deer that weighs up to 252 pounds (114 kg)!

COLOR

A Highland pony can be any of a wide assortment of colors. The coat may be liver chestnut, gray, black, brown, or bay. Highlands also come in a variety of duns, such as mouse, yellow, gray, and cream.

Many Highland ponies have a narrow stripe of color along the top of the back. They may also have stripes similar to a zebra's on their legs. Highland ponies should not have any white markings. However, a small star on the forehead is allowed.

Some Highland ponies get so dirty that you cannot tell what color they are. Still, grass-kept ponies should not be groomed daily. Mud keeps the skin and coat in good condition. But, daily grooming pleases your stabled pony and is a form of massage.

Worldwide, there are about 5,000 to 6,000 Highland ponies.

CARE

An owner is responsible for providing his or her Highland pony with good care. This means being kind and gentle. Most importantly, it means providing shelter.

Not all Highland ponies like stables. Another option is keeping it at pasture. For this, an owner needs a plot of land that is at least two acres (1 ha). It should be surrounded by a strong wooden fence with a wide, locking gate.

A Highland pony at pasture will also need shelter from the weather. A large, open barn works well for this. A layer of dry straw or wood shavings on the floor will make it comfortable for the pony.

Healthy feet are important. They should be looked at daily. Check that the horseshoes are in good shape. Remove any objects with a hoof pick. A **farrier** will need to trim your Highland's hooves about every six weeks.

Veterinary visits should occur once a year. The doctor will check the pony's teeth, eyes, and all-around health. A Highland pony should also receive shots to prevent it from getting diseases.

Highland ponies do not like to be alone. Make sure that your Highland can see other ponies.

FEEDING

A Highland pony kept at pasture still needs good food. Make sure quality grass is growing on the land where the pony grazes. And, keep the land free from harmful plants such as nettles and ragwort. These plants can be poisonous or cause stomach problems.

When grass is scarce, hay and haylage are good substitutes. Haylage is similar to moist hay. It is good for ponies in the winter. But, hay is a better choice because it is not as rich.

A Highland pony's diet needs to be watched. Highlands can eat too much food and become overweight. And, they are not used to rich foods. Clean water needs to be provided daily in a watering **trough**.

If your horse is stabled, it will need daily treats. Stabled Highland ponies like carrots, apples, and turnips. A grass-kept horse does not need additional food. It receives enough **nutrients** from the grass.

Shetland ponies are also found grazing in Scotland. Like Highlands, they can survive on rough pastures. They do not need much extra feeding.

THINGS HIGHLAND PONIES NEED

Highland ponies also require equipment, which is called tack. Use tack that fits well and keep it clean. Poorly fitting or dirty tack can irritate the pony's body or mouth, and cause other problems.

Saddles are a main piece of gear. A general purpose saddle is suitable for work such as **hacking** and cross-country work.

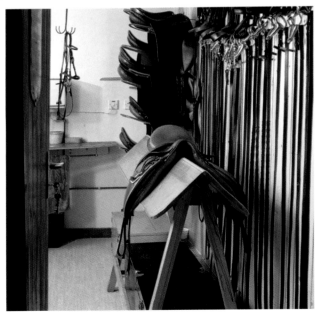

Many owners have a tack room to keep their tack organized and safe from moisture.

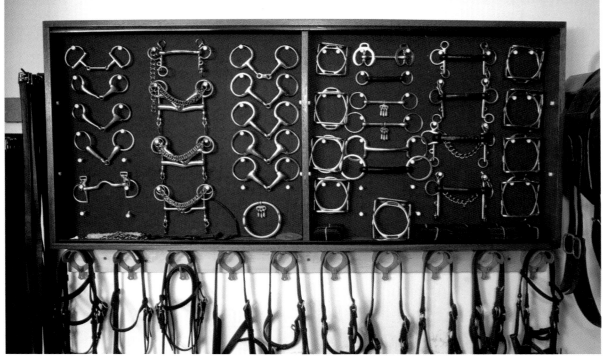

Tack can be expensive. Keeping your tack organized will keep it in good condition for a longer period of time.

The saddle should sit on top of a saddle cloth. This cloth cushions the pony's back and sides. It protects your Highland from the rubbing of the saddle.

Another piece of tack is the bridle. It directs the pony when being ridden. The bridle consists of leather straps that fit over the pony's head. Reins and a bit attach to the bridle. The bit is metal and placed in the mouth over the tongue.

How Highland Ponies Grow

A female Highland pony is **pregnant** for about 11 months. When she's ready to give birth, she needs a comfortable, private place. Most often, she has just one baby. The baby pony is called a foal.

A Highland foal should soon start drinking its mother's milk. This first milk has a lot of vitamins and other things a foal needs. Within a few hours, the foal will stand on its wobbly legs. By instinct, the foal follows its mother.

Soon, the foal will be running and playing. A Highland pony will want to trot and gallop. It uses up its energy quickly by playing. So, the foal needs to rest often. When the foal is about eight months old, it will be **weaned** from its mother.

You should introduce your foal to grooming and handling within a few days of its birth.

TRAINING

In a way, a Highland pony begins its training right after it is born. Its very first lesson is getting used to people. It must learn to allow humans to work with it.

The trainer will teach the pony slowly and patiently. When it is a few days old, the trainer will introduce the pony to a **halter**. This is an important first step. When it is two years old, the pony may get used to a saddle.

Some Highland ponies are trained to perform in horse shows.

At about three years old, your pony should start training on a long rein called a lunge rein. Your pony will be on one end with the trainer on the other end. The pony will learn to follow voice commands.

Once the pony is disciplined, it will learn to tolerate a rider on its back. The trainer will slowly introduce physical commands that go with voice commands.

Once a pony learns signals, it can be trained for a certain task. Many Highlands still trek and perform farmwork in the hills of Scotland. However, some people enjoy riding and showing them as well.

Highland ponies can jump up to about four feet (1 m) high. They can also run medium-length cross-country courses.

GLOSSARY

breed - a group of animals sharing the same appearance and characteristics. A breeder is a person who raises animals. Raising animals is often called breeding them.

farrier - a person who shoes horses.

hack - to ride a horse at an ordinary pace.

halter - a rope or strap for leading or restraining an animal.

muzzle - an animal's nose and jaws.

nutrient - a substance found in food and used in the body to promote growth, maintenance, and repair.

pregnant - having one or more babies growing within the body.

trough - a long, shallow container for the drinking water or feed of domestic animals.

wean - to accustom an animal to eat food other than its mother's milk.

WEB SITES

To learn more about Highland ponies, visit ABDO
Publishing Company on the World Wide Web at
www.abdopub.com. Web sites about these ponies are
featured on our Book Links page. These links are
routinely monitored and updated to provide the most
current information available.

INDEX

ML

10/0